I0710744

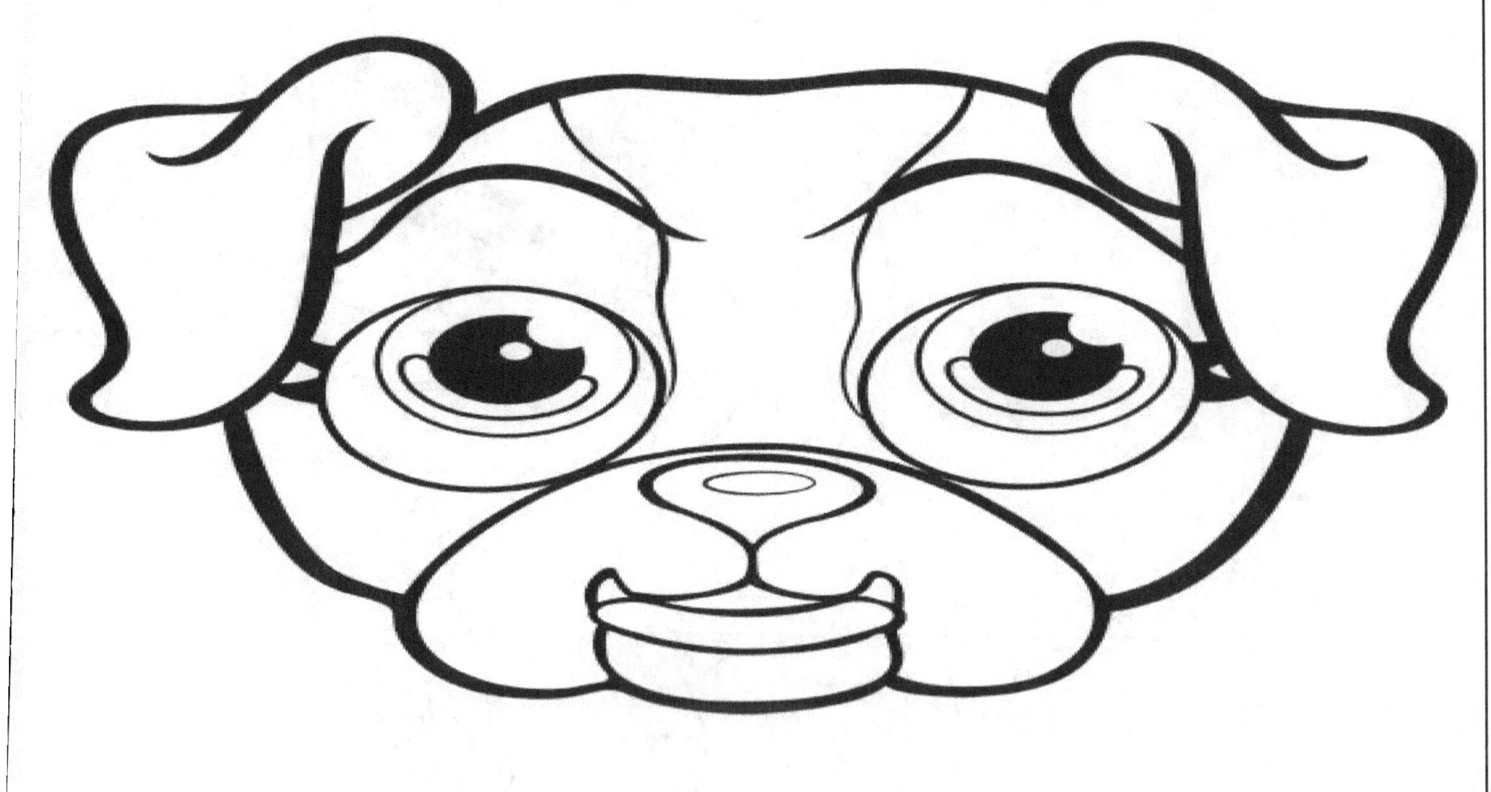

SPOT

D

Dog

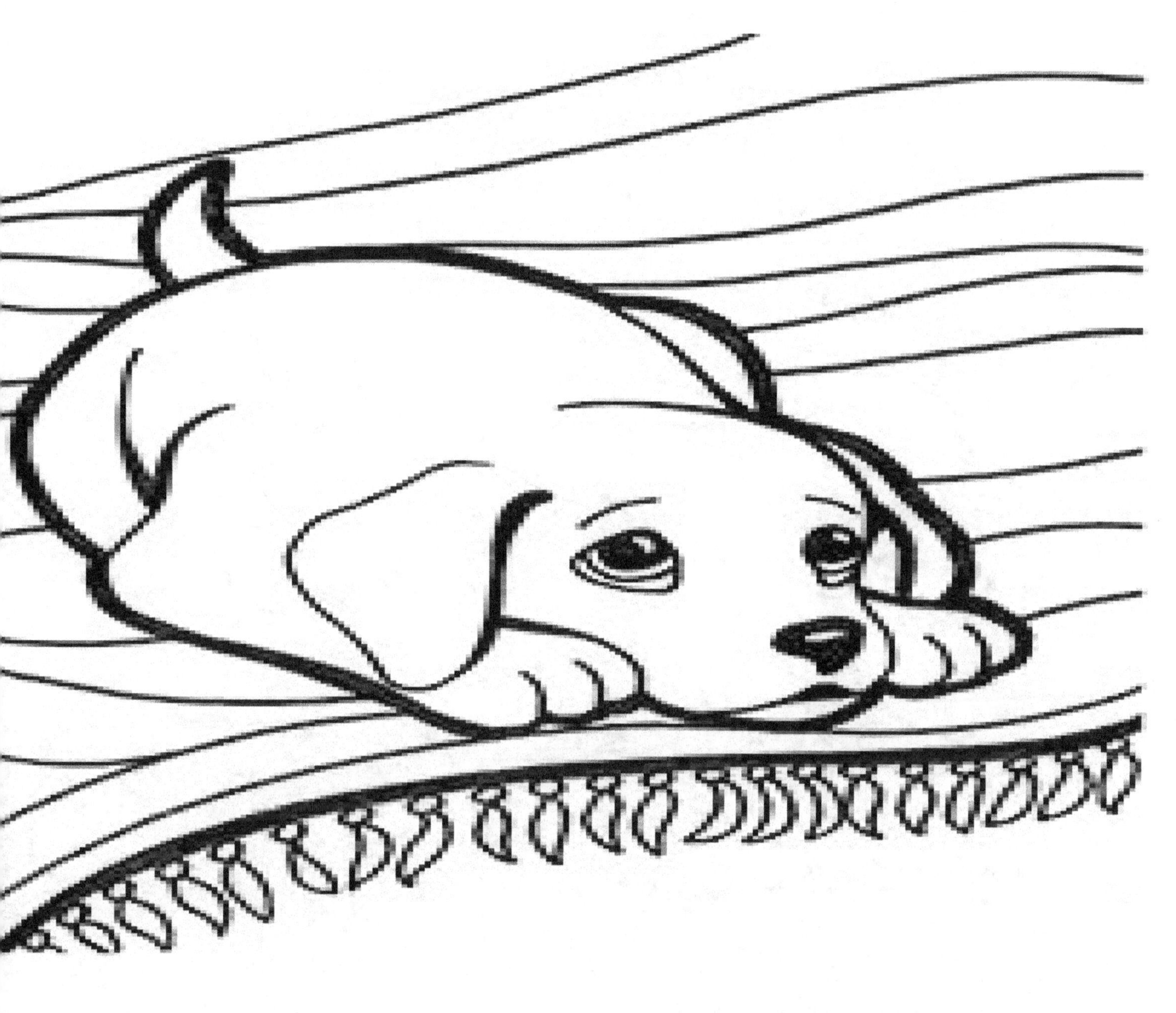

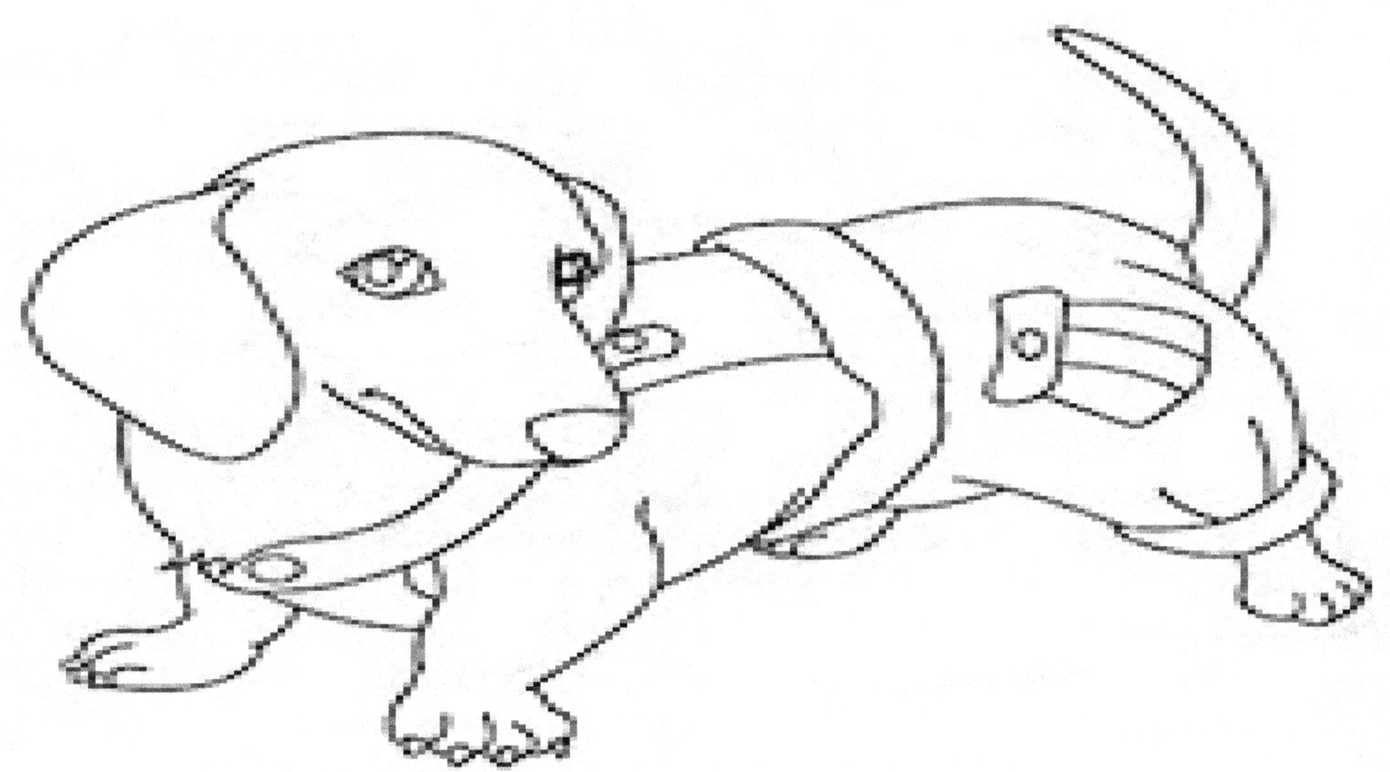

MOVERS

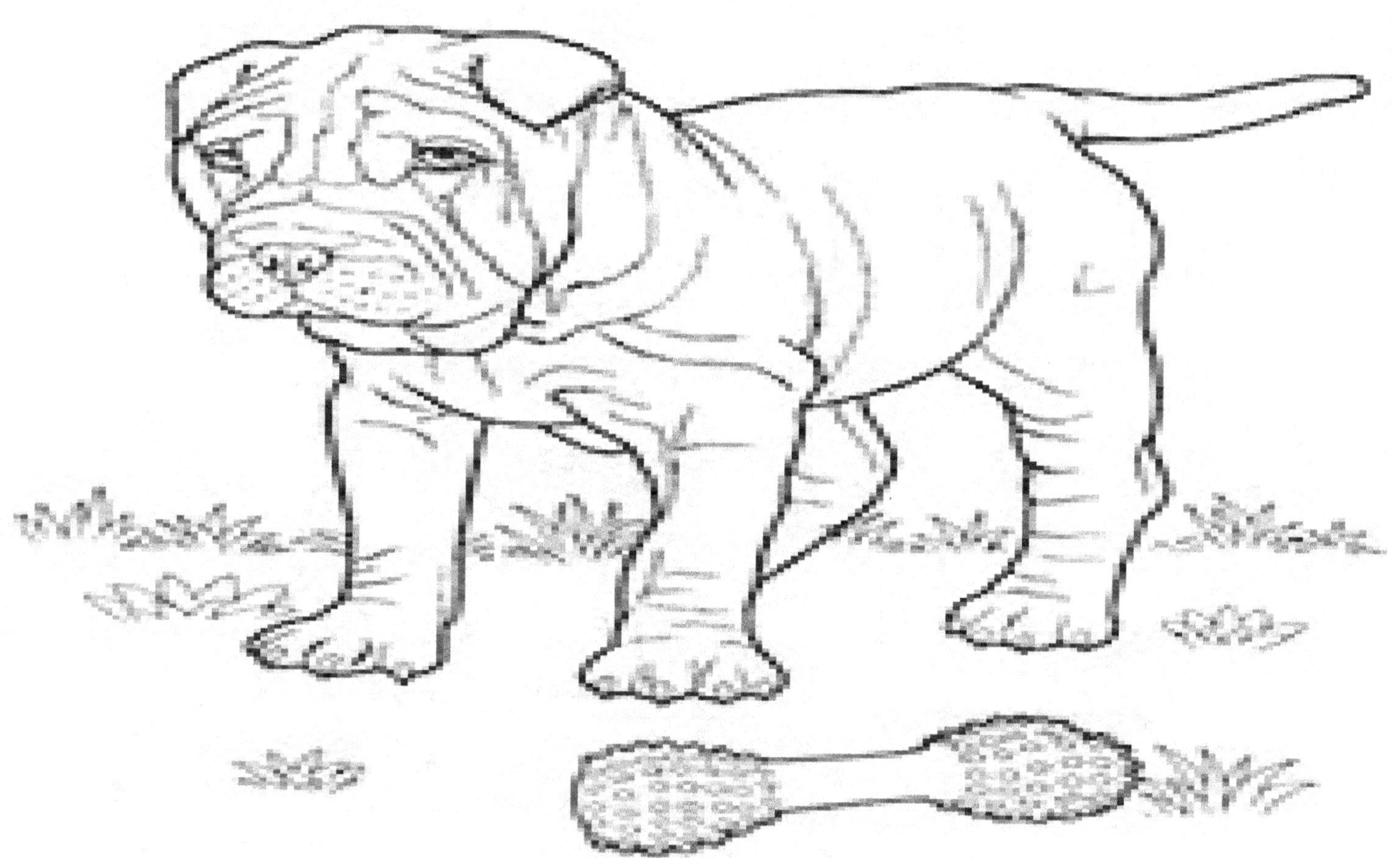

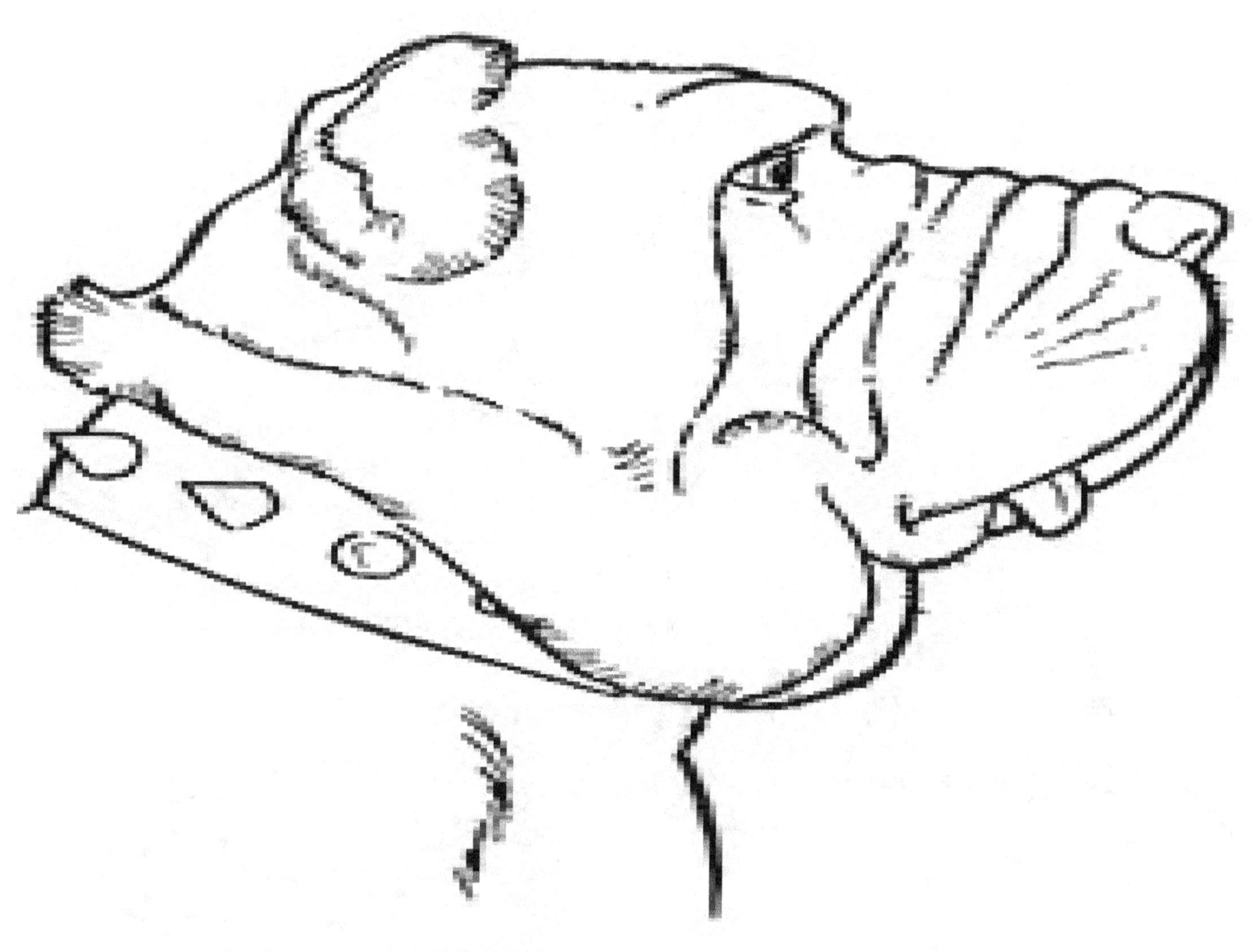

REX

www.ingramcontent.com/pod-product-compliance
Lightning Source LLC
Chambersburg PA
CBHW081444250726
48662CB00009B/2935